PYTHON CRASH FOR BEGINNERS

LEARNING PYTHON PROGRAMMING IN SEVEN DAYS

OLIVER LUCAS JR

TABLE OF CONTENTS

Chapter 10

Preface

Welcome to the exciting world of Python programming! This book is designed to be your companion on a journey from a complete beginner to a confident Python coder. Whether you're a student, a hobbyist, or someone looking to enhance your professional skillset, this book provides a structured and engaging path to mastering Python fundamentals.

Throughout this book, you'll gain a strong foundation in core Python concepts like variables, data types, operators, control flow statements, and functions. You'll delve into working with data structures like lists, tuples, and dictionaries, equipping you to organize and manipulate information effectively. We'll explore essential techniques for user input and output, allowing you to build interactive programs that respond to user interaction.

By the end of this book, you'll be able to write Python programs that can:

Perform calculations and automate tasks.

Analyze and manipulate data.

Create simple games and interactive applications.

Why Python?

Python is a versatile and powerful programming language, widely recognized for its:

Readability: Python's clear and concise syntax makes it easy to learn and understand, even for those with no prior programming experience.

Versatility: Python can be used for various applications, from web development and data science to scientific computing and automation.

Large and Supportive Community: Python boasts a vast and active community of developers, offering extensive learning resources, libraries, and frameworks to support your programming journey.

What This Book Offers:

This book adopts a practical and hands-on approach to learning Python. You'll learn by doing, with clear explanations followed by engaging exercises and challenges that solidify your understanding. Here's what you can expect:

Step-by-Step Learning: Each chapter builds upon the previous one, ensuring a smooth progression in your learning curve.

Clear Explanations: Complex concepts are broken down into easy-to-understand terms, aided by illustrative examples.

Interactive Exercises: Each chapter concludes with practice exercises that allow you to apply your newly acquired knowledge and test your skills.

Real-World Examples: Real-world scenarios and use cases are incorporated throughout the book to demonstrate the practical applications of Python.

Project-Based Learning: The final chapter guides you through building your first Python project, putting all your learned concepts into practice.

How to Use This Book:

This book is designed to be flexible and adaptable to your learning style. Here are some suggestions to optimize your learning experience:

Read Actively: Don't just skim through the text. Engage with the explanations, take notes, and ask yourself questions.

Practice Regularly: The key to mastering Python is consistent practice. Dedicating time each day or week to work on the exercises and challenges is crucial.

Experiment and Explore: Don't be afraid to experiment with the code provided. Try modifying the examples and see what happens. This hands-on exploration will deepen your understanding.

Seek Help When Needed: If you encounter challenges, don't hesitate to consult the wealth of online resources available for Python learners. There are forums, communities, and tutorials that can provide additional support.

I believe that anyone with dedication and a willingness to learn can master Python. This book is your roadmap to success. So, buckle up, get ready to code, and embark on a rewarding journey into the world of Python programming!

Chapter 1

Welcome to the World of Python (Day 1)

This chapter will serve as your introduction to the exciting world of Python programming! We'll unveil what Python is and why it's a fantastic choice for beginners and early starters like you.

1.1: Unveiling the Python Programming Language: What is Python? Why Choose Python? (Benefits and Applications)

Welcome to the world of Python programming! In this section, we'll dive into what Python is and explore the reasons why it's an excellent choice for beginners and early starters like yourself.

What is Python?

Python is a high-level, general-purpose programming language. This means it's designed to be easy to read and understand, unlike some machine languages that require complex codes. Think of Python as a powerful tool that allows you to give instructions to a computer in a clear and concise way.

Here are some key characteristics of Python:

Easy to Learn: Python's syntax is known for its readability, resembling everyday English. This makes it a breeze to grasp the fundamentals compared to other programming languages.

Versatile: Python's applications are vast. You can use it for web development, data analysis, machine learning, automation tasks, and even scientific computing.

Free and Open-Source: Python is completely free to use and modify, with a large and supportive community constantly developing new libraries and tools.

Extensive Libraries: Python boasts a massive collection of libraries, which are pre-written code modules that provide functionalities for various tasks. This saves you time from writing everything from scratch and allows you to focus on solving problems.

Why Choose Python? (Benefits and Applications)

There are numerous reasons why Python is an ideal language for beginners and early learners:

Gentle Learning Curve: Python's beginner-friendly syntax makes it easier to grasp programming concepts without feeling overwhelmed.

In-Demand Skills: Python is one of the most sought-after programming languages in the job market, opening doors to exciting career opportunities.

Wide Range of Applications: With Python, you can explore various fields like web development, data science, and automation, giving you flexibility in your career path.

Active Community: The Python community is extensive and welcoming, offering a wealth of online resources, tutorials, and forums to help you on your learning journey.

Let's look at some specific applications of Python to spark your interest:

Web Development: Python powers popular web frameworks like Django, making it a valuable tool for building dynamic websites and applications.

Data Science: Python is a leader in data science due to powerful libraries like NumPy and pandas for data analysis, manipulation, and visualization.

Machine Learning: Python is a go-to language for machine learning with libraries like TensorFlow and scikit-learn, allowing you to build intelligent systems and algorithms.

Automation: Python excels at automating repetitive tasks, saving you time and effort. You can automate web scraping, data processing, and even file management.

By choosing Python, you're not just learning a programming language; you're unlocking a gateway to a world of possibilities! In the following sections, we'll guide you through setting up your Python environment and writing your first program. So buckle up and get ready to explore the exciting world of Python coding!

1.2: Setting Up Your Python Environment:

Now that you're excited about the world of Python, let's get your environment ready for coding! This section will guide you through installing Python on your computer and introduce tools you'll use to write your programs.

Installing Python on Your Computer (Step-by-Step Guide):

Head to the Official Website: Visit the official Python downloads page at https://www.python.org/downloads/.

Choose the Right Version: For beginners, it's recommended to download the latest stable version of Python 3. You'll see options for Windows, macOS, and Linux.

Download the Installer: Select the appropriate installer file for your operating system (Windows typically uses an executable file).

Run the Installer: Double-click the downloaded installer file and follow the on-screen instructions. It's generally recommended to keep the default installation options unless you have specific requirements.

Verify Installation (Optional): Once the installation is complete, you can verify it by opening a command prompt or terminal window and typing `python --version` (or `python3` on some systems). If successful, you'll see the installed Python version displayed.

Introduction to a Python IDE or Text Editor:

An Integrated Development Environment (IDE) or a text editor is where you'll write your Python code. Here's a quick breakdown of both options:

IDE (Integrated Development Environment): IDEs offer a comprehensive set of features for writing, running, and debugging Python code. They often include features like code completion, syntax highlighting, debugging tools, and project management capabilities. Popular choices include PyCharm, Visual Studio Code, and IDLE (which comes bundled with the Python installation).

Text Editor: Text editors are more basic tools that allow you to write and edit plain text files, including Python code. They are lightweight and offer flexibility for experienced programmers. However, they may lack some advanced features compared to IDEs. Popular text editors include Sublime Text, Atom, and Notepad++ (with appropriate plugins).

Choosing Between IDE and Text Editor:

For beginners, starting with an IDE is recommended. The user-friendly interface and features like code completion can significantly improve your learning experience. As you gain confidence, you can explore text editors for a more customized coding experience.

In the next section, we'll navigate the Python environment you just set up and write your first program!

1.3: Navigating the Python Playground:

Welcome to the Python playground! Now that you have Python installed and your chosen IDE or text editor ready, it's time to write your first program. Here, we'll cover the basics of Python syntax, write some simple code examples, and show you how to run and see the results!

Understanding Basic Syntax:

Python code is built using clear and concise instructions. Here are some fundamental elements you'll encounter:

Print Statements: The `print()` function allows you to display output on the screen. Anything placed inside the parentheses will be printed.

Variables: Variables act like containers that store data you can use in your programs. You can give them meaningful names to represent the information they hold.

Writing Your First Python Program (Simple Code Examples):

Let's write a few basic programs to get you started:

Example 1: Printing Hello World

```python
Python

print("Hello, World!")
```

This classic program simply prints the message "Hello, World!" on the screen.

Example 2: Using a Variable

Python

```python
message = "Welcome to Python Programming!"
print(message)
```

Here, we create a variable named `message` and assign it a string value. Then, we use the `print()` function to display the contents of the variable.

Running Your Code and Seeing Results:

Now that you have your code written, it's time to run it and see the magic happen! The specific steps will vary depending on your chosen IDE or text editor. Here's a general guideline:

Save Your Code: Give your program a descriptive filename (e.g., `hello_world.py`).

Run the Program: In your IDE or text editor, look for the option to run the Python script. This might be a button or a menu option.

Once you run the program, you should see the output displayed in the console window or a designated output area within your IDE.

Congratulations! You've just written and run your first Python programs. These are small steps, but they mark the beginning of your exciting coding journey!

As you progress through this course, we'll delve deeper into Python syntax, explore various data types, and build more complex programs. We'll equip you with the skills to tackle real-world problems and unlock the power of Python programming!

Chapter 2

Mastering the Essentials (Day 1 & 2)

Welcome back, aspiring Python programmers! In this chapter, we'll solidify your foundation by delving into the essential building blocks of Python. We'll cover data types, operators, and user input, equipping you to create more intricate programs.

2.1: Working with Variables: Storing and Manipulating Data

Variables are the workhorses of any programming language, and Python is no exception. They act like containers that hold data you can use throughout your programs. Understanding how to work with variables effectively is essential for building any Python application.

Assigning Values:

In Python, you assign values to variables using the assignment operator (=). Here's the basic syntax:

Python

```
variable_name = value
```

For example:

Python

```
name = "Alice"
age = 30
```

```
greeting = "Hello, World!"
```

In this code snippet, we've created three variables:

`name` stores the string value "Alice".

`age` stores the integer value 30.

`greeting` stores the string value "Hello, World!".

Choosing Meaningful Names:

It's crucial to choose descriptive names for your variables. These names should reflect the data they hold, making your code easier to read and understand for yourself and others. Python follows the convention of using snake_case for variable names, which means using lowercase letters with underscores to separate words (e.g., total_score, shopping_cart).

Data Types: The Clothes Your Variables Wear

Imagine variables like boxes; they can hold different types of things. In Python, data types define the kind of information a variable can store. Here are some fundamental data types you'll encounter frequently:

Numbers:

Integers (int): Represent whole numbers, positive, negative, or zero (e.g., -5, 10, 100).

Floats (float): Represent numbers with decimals (e.g., 3.14159, -2.5).

Strings (str): Represent sequences of text characters. You can enclose strings in either single quotes (') or double quotes ("). Examples: "This is a string" and 'This is also a string'.

Booleans (bool): Represent logical values: True or False. These are typically used in conditional statements to make decisions based on certain conditions.

Using Variables in Your Programs:

Once you've assigned values to variables, you can use them throughout your code. Here are some common ways to manipulate variables:

Performing Calculations: You can use variables in arithmetic expressions along with operators (+, -, *, /) to perform calculations. For example:

Python

```python
total_cost = price * quantity
```

String Concatenation: The + operator can be used to combine strings.

Python

```python
full_name = first_name + " " + last_name
```

Reassigning Values: You can change the value stored in a variable using the assignment operator again.

Python

```python
score = 75
score += 10  # Increase the score by 10
```

Remember: It's generally good practice to avoid reassigning values to variables with different data types unless you have a specific reason to do so. This helps maintain code clarity and avoids potential errors.

By mastering variables and data types, you'll lay a strong foundation for building more intricate Python programs. In the next section, we'll delve deeper into understanding the different data types Python offers and how to work with them effectively.

2.2: Understanding Data Types: Numbers, Text, Booleans, and More

In Chapter 2.1, we explored the concept of variables and how they act like containers to store data in your Python programs. Now, let's delve deeper into the different data types that define the kind of information a variable can hold.

Numbers: Representing Quantities

Python offers two primary data types for storing numerical data:

Integers (int): These represent whole numbers, both positive, negative, and zero. Examples include -5, 10, and 100.

Floats (float): These represent numbers with decimals, allowing for more precise calculations. Examples include 3.14159, -2.5, and 1.2e+3 (scientific notation for 1200).

Performing Calculations with Numbers:

You can use variables of these data types in arithmetic expressions along with operators (+, -, *, /) to perform calculations:

Python

```python
# Addition and subtraction
total_price = price_of_item1 + price_of_item2

# Multiplication and division
distance = speed * time
average = total / number_of_items

# Integer division (floor division) and modulo
(remainder)
quotient = 10 // 3    # quotient will be 3
(discards the remainder)
remainder = 10 % 3  # remainder will be 1
```

Strings: Sequences of Text Characters

Strings represent any combination of text characters enclosed in either single quotes (') or double quotes ("). Examples:

"Hello, World!"

'This is a string with single quotes.'

String Operations:

Python provides various built-in functions for manipulating strings:

Concatenation: The + operator combines strings to form a new string.

Python

```python
full_name = first_name + " " + last_name
```

String Slicing: You can extract specific portions of a string using indexing and slicing. Square brackets `[]` are used for this purpose.

```
Python
```

```python
name = "Alice"
first_letter = name[0]   # first_letter will be
"A"
substring = name[2:5]   # substring will be "ice"
(extracts characters from index 2 to 4, excluding
index 4)
```

Booleans: True or False

Booleans are fundamental for making decisions in your programs. They represent logical values: True or False. These are typically used in conditional statements to control the flow of your program based on certain conditions.

```
Python
```

```python
is_sunny = True
is_finished = False
```

Using Comparisons with Booleans:

Comparison operators like $==$ (equal to), $!=$ (not equal to), $<$ (less than), $>$ (greater than), $<=$ (less than or equal to), and $>=$ (greater than or equal to) return True or False based on the comparison result.

```python
Python

x = 5
y = 3
is_greater = x > y  # is_greater will be True
```

Remember: Data types play a crucial role in Python. Understanding the different data types ensures you store and manipulate data appropriately, leading to well-functioning and efficient programs. As we progress through this course, we'll encounter more complex data types like lists and dictionaries, expanding your ability to manage information in your Python code.

2.3: Operators in Action: Performing Calculations and Comparisons

In programming, operators are symbols that perform specific operations on data. They are the workhorses that allow you to manipulate data within your Python programs. In this section, we'll explore the essential operators used for calculations and comparisons.

1. Arithmetic Operators:

These operators perform mathematical calculations on numerical data (integers and floats). Here are the common ones:

Addition (+)

Subtraction (−)

Multiplication (*)

Division (/)

Note: Regular division results in a float, even if the operands are integers. For integer division (floor division), use the // operator, which discards the remainder.

Modulo (%) This operator calculates the remainder after a division operation.

Examples:

```Python
total_cost = price * quantity
average_score = total_score / number_of_students
remainder = 10 % 3  # remainder will be 1
```

2. Comparison Operators:

These operators compare values and return True or False based on the comparison result. They are essential for making decisions in your programs using conditional statements. Here are the common comparison operators:

Equal to (==)

Not equal to (!=)

Greater than (>)

Less than (<)

Greater than or equal to (>=)

Less than or equal to (<=)

Examples:

```python
Python

age = 25
is_adult = age >= 18  # is_adult will be True

name1 = "Alice"
name2 = "Bob"
are_equal = name1 == name2  # are_equal will be
False
```

3. Logical Operators (Optional for Day 2):

These operators combine conditional statements and allow for more complex decision-making logic. We'll cover them in more detail later (potentially in Day 3 or a dedicated section), but here's a brief overview:

and: Returns True only if both conditions are True.

or: Returns True if at least one condition is True.

not: Inverts the truth value of a condition (True becomes False and vice versa).

By effectively combining these operators with variables and data types, you can perform various calculations, comparisons, and control the flow of your Python programs. The next sections will explore user input and how you can integrate it into your code, making your programs more interactive. However, understanding logical operators might be more relevant for controlling program flow in later chapters, so you can decide if you want to cover them now (Day 2) or introduce them later.

Chapter 3

Conquering Control Flow (Day 2)

Welcome back, Python warriors! In the previous chapters, we mastered variables, data types, and operators, equipping us to perform calculations and manipulate data. This chapter delves into a fundamental concept in programming: control flow. We'll explore conditional statements and loops, allowing your programs to make decisions and repeat tasks efficiently.

3.1: Making Decisions with Conditional Statements: if, elif, and else

Conditional statements, also known as decision-making structures, are fundamental to controlling the flow of your Python programs. They allow your programs to evaluate conditions and execute different code blocks based on the results. Here, we'll explore the power of if, elif (else if), and else statements:

The if Statement:

The if statement checks a condition. If the condition evaluates to True, the indented code block following the colon (:) is executed.

Python

```python
if condition:
    # Code to execute if the condition is True
```

Example:

Python

```python
age = 25
if age >= 18:
    print("You are an adult.")
```

In this example, the `if` statement checks if the value of `age` is greater than or equal to 18. If it is, the indented code (`print("You are an adult.")`) is executed.

The `elif` Statement (Optional for Day 2):

The `elif` statement (else if) allows you to check multiple conditions sequentially. It's useful when you have more than two possible outcomes.

Python

```python
if condition1:
    # Code to execute if condition1 is True
elif condition2:
    # Code to execute if condition1 is False and
condition2 is True
```

You can chain multiple `elif` statements to handle various scenarios.

Example (can be introduced later):

Python

```python
grade = 85
if grade >= 90:
    print("Excellent!")
elif grade >= 80:
    print("Great job!")
else:
    print("Keep practicing!")
```

Here, the program first checks if `grade` is greater than or equal to 90. If not, it moves on to the `elif` statement to see if `grade` is greater than or equal to 80.

The `else` Statement:

The `else` statement provides an optional code block that executes only if none of the preceding conditions in `if` or `elif` statements are True.

Python

```python
if condition:
# Code to execute if the condition is True
else:
# Code to execute if the condition is False
```

Example:

Python

```
is_raining = False
if is_raining:
print("Take an umbrella.")
else:
print("Enjoy the sunshine!")
```

In this case, if `is_raining` is False, the `else` block executes, and the program prints "Enjoy the sunshine!"

Using Comparisons with Conditional Statements:

Remember the comparison operators (`==`, `!=`, `<`, `>`, `<=`, `>=`) we learned in Chapter 2.3? These operators are essential for writing effective conditional statements. You can compare values, strings, or even booleans to make decisions within your program.

By mastering these conditional statements, you'll equip your Python programs to make informed decisions based on different conditions, adding a layer of interactivity and complexity to your code. In the next section, we'll delve into loops, another powerful concept for controlling program flow.

3.2: Looping Through Data: for Loops and While Loops

In programming, loops are essential tools for repeated execution of tasks. Python offers two primary loop types: `for` loops and `while` loops, allowing you to automate processes and iterate over sequences of data efficiently.

The `for` Loop:

The `for` loop is ideal for iterating over a sequence of items like a list, string, or tuple. It executes a block of code for each item in the sequence.

Python

```python
for item in sequence:

# Code to execute for each item in the sequence
```

Example:

Python

```python
fruits = ["apple", "banana", "cherry"]

for fruit in fruits:

print(fruit)
```

In this example, the `for` loop iterates through the `fruits` list, assigning each fruit ("apple", "banana", and "cherry") to the variable `fruit` one at a time within the loop. The indented code block (`print(fruit)`) then prints each fruit name.

The `while` Loop:

The `while` loop keeps executing a block of code as long as a certain condition remains True. This allows for repetitive tasks until a specific condition is met.

Python

```
while condition:

    # Code to execute as long as the condition is
True
```

Example:

Python

```
count = 0

while count < 5:

print("Count:", count)

count += 1  # Increment the count by 1
```

Here, the `while` loop continues to print "Count:" followed by the current value of `count` as long as `count` is less than 5. After each iteration, `count` is incremented by 1 using `count += 1`, eventually causing the condition to become False (when `count` reaches 5) and terminating the loop.

Understanding Indentation:

Remember that indentation is crucial in Python for defining code blocks. The indented lines following the `for` or `while` statement belong to the loop's body and execute repeatedly until the loop's condition is no longer met.

Choosing the Right Loop:

Use `for` loops when you know the exact number of times you want to iterate or when you're working with a sequence of items.

Use `while` loops when you need to repeat a task until a certain condition is met (and you may not know the exact number of iterations beforehand).

By mastering these loops, you'll be able to automate repetitive tasks in your Python programs, making them more efficient and powerful. In the next section, we'll explore some best practices for using loops effectively.

3.3: Building Blocks of Programs: Indentation and Code Blocks

Absolutely, indentation is a fundamental concept in Python, and understanding it is essential for writing correct and readable code.

Indentation: The Backbone of Python's Code Blocks

Unlike some other programming languages that use curly braces ({}) to define code blocks, Python relies on indentation to structure your code. The indentation level determines which lines of code belong to a particular loop, conditional statement, or function. Consistent and proper indentation is vital for Python to interpret your code correctly.

Maintaining Readable Indentation:

Four-Space Indentation: As a standard practice, use four spaces for each indentation level. This improves readability and maintains consistency throughout your codebase.

Indentation Scope: The indented code block belongs to the preceding statement (like `if`, `for`, or `while`). The lines of code within the indentation define the actions to be executed repeatedly or conditionally.

Examples of Indentation:

Python

```python
# if statement with indented code block
if age >= 18:
    print("You are an adult.")

# for loop iterating over a list
fruits = ["apple", "banana", "cherry"]
for fruit in fruits:
    print(fruit) * 2   # Notice the indented line
belongs to the for loop

# while loop with multiple indented lines
count = 0
while count < 5:
    print("Count:", count)
        count += 1    # Increment count (notice
indentation)
```

Errors Caused by Improper Indentation:

Incorrect indentation can lead to errors or unexpected behavior in your Python programs. Python interprets the indentation level to determine the code block structure. Mixing spaces and tabs for indentation is strictly not recommended as it can cause issues.

Benefits of Consistent Indentation:

Improved Readability: Consistent indentation makes your code visually easier to understand, especially for complex programs with nested loops and conditional statements.

Fewer Errors: Proper indentation reduces the likelihood of errors caused by misplaced code blocks.

Maintainability: Well-indented code is easier to maintain and modify in the future, both for yourself and others.

By following these indentation guidelines, you'll write Python code that is clear, correct, and easier to manage as your programs become more intricate. In the next chapter, we'll delve into functions, another essential concept for building well-structured and reusable Python programs.

Chapter 4

Organizing Your Code with Functions (Day 3)

Welcome back, Python champions! In the previous chapters, we conquered variables, data types, operators, control flow with conditional statements and loops, and the importance of indentation. This chapter introduces functions, a powerful concept in Python that allows you to organize your code, improve reusability, and enhance readability.

4.1: What are Functions?

Functions are reusable blocks of code that perform specific tasks. They group related instructions under a meaningful name, promoting code modularity and maintainability. Here's the basic structure of a function:

Python

```python
def function_name(parameters):
    """ Docstring (optional) """
    # Code to be executed
    return value  # Optional return statement
```

`def` **keyword:** This keyword declares the beginning of a function definition.

`function_name`: Choose a descriptive name that reflects the function's purpose (e.g., `calculate_area`, `greet_user`).

`parameters` **(optional):** These are placeholders for values that will be passed to the function when it's called. Parameters are enclosed in parentheses and separated by commas.

`Docstring` **(optional):** A brief explanation of what the function does, improving code readability and understanding.

Indented code block: The indented lines within the function body define the instructions the function executes.

`return` **statement (optional):** This statement returns a value from the function to the code that called it. If no `return` statement is present, the function implicitly returns `None`.

Understanding Functions with an Analogy:

Think of functions like recipes in a cookbook. A recipe has a name (function_name), a list of ingredients (parameters), and cooking instructions (code block). You can use the same recipe (function) multiple times with different ingredients (arguments) to create different dishes (function outputs).

Benefits of Using Functions:

Code Reusability: Functions allow you to write a block of code once and use it multiple times throughout your program or even in other Python programs. This saves time and effort.

Improved Readability: By breaking down complex logic into smaller, well-defined functions, your code becomes easier to understand and maintain.

Modular Design: Functions promote modular programming, where you can organize your code into smaller, manageable units. This makes your programs more scalable and easier to modify.

We'll delve deeper into defining and calling functions in the next section, and explore how they can be used to make your Python code more efficient and organized.

4.2: Defining and Calling Functions

Now that we understand the concept of functions, let's see how to define and call them in Python to make our programs more modular and reusable.

Defining Functions:

The `def` keyword marks the beginning of a function definition. Here's the general structure:

Python

```
def function_name(parameters):
    """ Docstring (optional) """
    # Code to be executed (function body)
    return value  # Optional return statement
```

`function_name`: Choose a descriptive name that reflects the function's purpose (e.g., `calculate_area`, `greet_user`).

`parameters` **(optional):** These are placeholders for values that will be passed to the function when it's called. Parameters are enclosed in parentheses and separated by commas.

`Docstring` **(optional):** A brief explanation of what the function does, improving code readability and understanding.

Indented code block: The indented lines within the function body define the instructions the function executes.

`return` **statement (optional):** This statement returns a value from the function to the code that called it. If no `return` statement is present, the function implicitly returns `None`.

Example:

Python

```python
def greet(name):
    """ Prints a greeting message. """
    print("Hello,", name + "!")
```

In this example, we define a function named `greet` that takes one parameter, `name`. The indented code block contains the `print` statement that constructs and displays a greeting message using the provided name.

Calling Functions:

Once you've defined a function, you can call it from anywhere in your code to execute its instructions. Here's the syntax:

Python

```python
function_name(arguments)
```

`function_name`: The name you assigned to your function when you defined it.

`arguments`: The actual values you pass to the function, corresponding to the defined parameters. These are enclosed in parentheses and separated by commas.

Example:

```python
Python

greet("Alice")    # Calling the function with an
argument
```

When we call `greet("Alice")`, the value "Alice" is passed as an argument to the function, replacing the `name` parameter within the function's body. This results in the following output:

```
Hello, Alice!
```

Key Points:

The number of arguments you pass to a function must match the number of parameters defined in the function.

Arguments are evaluated when the function is called, and their values are assigned to the corresponding parameters within the function.

By effectively using functions, you can break down complex tasks into smaller, manageable units. This improves code organization, readability, and maintainability in your Python programs. In the next section, we'll explore the advantages of using functions in more detail.

4.3: Advantages of Using Functions

Functions are fundamental building blocks in Python programming, offering numerous benefits that make your code more efficient, readable, and maintainable. Here's a closer look at some of the key advantages:

1. Code Reusability:

Imagine you need to calculate the area of a rectangle multiple times throughout your program. Without functions, you'd write the same calculation code repeatedly. Functions come to the rescue! By defining a function like `calculate_area(length, width)` that encapsulates the area calculation logic, you can reuse this function wherever you need to calculate rectangular area. This saves you time and effort, and avoids the potential for errors caused by copy-pasting code with slight modifications.

2. Improved Readability:

As your programs grow in complexity, well-defined functions enhance readability. Functions group related code blocks under descriptive names, making it easier to understand what each part of your code does. Instead of deciphering lengthy code sections, you can focus on the function names and their purposes. This improves code maintainability for both yourself and others collaborating on the project.

3. Modular Design:

Functions promote a modular programming approach. By breaking down your program into smaller, self-contained functions, you create a more organized code structure. This modularity makes your code easier to understand, test, debug, and modify. If you need to change the functionality of a specific task, you can modify the relevant function without affecting other parts of your program.

4. Increased Maintainability:

As you or others work on your codebase in the future, clear and well-defined functions make it easier to grasp the program's logic and modify it as needed. Functions act as documented code units, explaining their purpose and functionality through their names and docstrings. This reduces maintenance time and effort in the long run.

5. Namespaces and Reduced Risk of Errors:

Functions create their own local namespaces, preventing naming conflicts with variables from other parts of your code. This helps to avoid errors caused by accidentally using the same name for different variables.

By leveraging these advantages, functions become essential tools for writing well-structured, efficient, and maintainable Python programs. In the next section, we'll delve into different function types and how you can return values from functions to use their outputs in other parts of your code.

4.4: Parameters and Arguments: Passing Data to Functions

In Python, functions can accept parameters, acting like placeholders for data you pass to the function when you call it. These parameters allow you to customize the function's behavior based on the provided values.

Understanding Parameters and Arguments:

Parameters: These are variables defined within the function's parentheses during its definition. They act as placeholders waiting to be filled with actual values when the function is called.

Arguments: These are the actual values you pass to the function when you call it. They are provided in the function call's parentheses, corresponding to the defined parameters.

Example:

Python

```python
def calculate_area(length, width):
    """ Calculates the area of a rectangle. """
    area = length * width
    return area

rectangle_area = calculate_area(5, 3)  # Calling the function with arguments
print("Area of the rectangle:", rectangle_area)
```

Here, the `calculate_area` function takes two parameters, `length` and `width`. When we call the function with `calculate_area(5, 3)`, the values 5 and 3 are passed as arguments, which are then assigned to the `length` and `width` parameters within the function's body. The function calculates the area using these values and returns the result.

Key Points:

The number of arguments you pass to a function must match the number of parameters defined in the function definition.

The order of the arguments should match the order of the parameters.

Arguments are evaluated when the function is called, and their values are assigned to the corresponding parameters within the function.

Using Default Arguments (Optional for Day 3):

Parameters can have default values, which are provided within the function definition itself. If no argument is passed for a parameter with a default value during the function call, the default value is used.

Example:

Python

```python
def greet(name="World"):
  """ Prints a greeting message. """
  print("Hello,", name + "!")

greet()  # Calling the function without arguments
```

In this example, the `greet` function has a parameter `name` with a default value of "World". If we call the function without providing an argument, the default value "World" is used for the `name` parameter.

Benefits of Using Parameters and Arguments:

Flexibility: Parameters allow you to make functions adaptable to different inputs, enabling them to handle various scenarios.

Code Reusability: By using parameters, you can write functions that can be reused with different sets of data, promoting code reusability.

Readability: Parameters with descriptive names enhance code readability, as they clearly indicate the type of data expected by the function.

Parameters and arguments are essential concepts in function usage. By effectively using them, you can create versatile and reusable functions that form the foundation of well-structured Python programs. In the next section, we'll explore different types of functions and how you can return values from them to use their outputs in other parts of your code.

Chapter 5

Working with Lists: Powerful Data Collections (Day 3 & 4)

Welcome back, Python warriors! In the previous chapters, we conquered variables, data types, operators, control flow with conditional statements and loops, and the importance of functions. This chapter dives into lists, a fundamental data structure in Python that allows you to store and manage collections of items in an ordered sequence.

5.1: Introduction to Lists

Lists are fundamental data structures in Python that allow you to store and manage collections of items in an ordered sequence. They are versatile and can hold various data types like numbers, strings, or even other lists (nested lists) within a single list.

Creating Lists:

You can create lists using square brackets `[]` and separate elements with commas. Here's the basic syntax:

Python

```
my_list = [element1, element2, ..., elementN]
```

Example:

Python

```python
fruits = ["apple", "banana", "cherry"]
numbers = [1, 2, 3, 4, 5]
mixed_data = [3.14, True, None, "hello"]
```

In these examples:

`fruits` is a list containing three strings representing fruits.

`numbers` is a list containing five integer values.

`mixed_data` is a list demonstrating that lists can hold elements of different data types.

Key Points:

Lists are mutable, meaning you can modify their content after creation (we'll cover this in later sections).

The order of elements in a list is important. The first element inserted into the list has index 0, the second element has index 1, and so on. This order matters when you access or modify elements within the list.

Accessing Elements in Lists:

You can access elements in a list using their index, which starts from 0. Here's how:

Python

```python
# Accessing the first element
first_item = my_list[0]

# Accessing the last element
last_item = my_list[-1]    # Negative indexing
starts from the end (-1 is last)
```

```
# Accessing an element in the middle
middle_item = my_list[2]  # Assuming the list has
at least 3 elements
```

Understanding IndexError:

If you try to access an element using an index that's out of bounds (less than 0 or greater than or equal to the list length), you'll get an `IndexError`. It's essential to ensure you use valid indices when accessing elements.

5.2: Modifying Lists

Lists are mutable in Python, which means you can change their content after they are created. This flexibility makes them powerful for storing and manipulating collections of data. Here, we'll explore some common methods for modifying lists:

Adding Elements:

`append(element)`: This method adds a new element to the end of the list.

Python

```
fruits = ["apple", "banana"]
fruits.append("cherry")   # Modifies the fruits
list
print(fruits)    # Output:  ["apple",  "banana",
"cherry"]
```

`insert(index, element)`: This method inserts a new element at a specific index within the list.

Python

```python
my_list = [1, 3, 5]
my_list.insert(1, 2)  # Insert 2 at index 1
print(my_list)  # Output: [1, 2, 3, 5]
```

Removing Elements:

`remove(element)`: This method removes the first occurrence of a specified element from the list.

Python

```python
my_list = [1, 2, 3, 2, 4]
my_list.remove(2)  # Removes the first occurrence
of 2
print(my_list)  # Output: [1, 3, 2, 4]
```

Important Note: `remove` only removes the first occurrence. If the element appears multiple times, only the first one is removed.

`pop(index)`: This method removes the element at a specified index from the list and returns the removed element. If no index is provided, it removes and returns the last element by default.

Python

```python
numbers = [10, 20, 30, 40]
```

```
removed_element  =  numbers.pop(1)   #  Removes
element at index 1 (20)
print(numbers)  # Output: [10, 30, 40]
print(removed_element)  # Output: 20
```

Be Cautious with `pop()`: Using `pop()` without an argument can lead to unexpected behavior if the list is empty, potentially causing an `IndexError`. It's generally safer to use `pop()` with a specific index or as a last resort.

Extending Lists:

`extend(iterable)`: This method appends all the elements from an iterable (like another list or a string) to the end of the original list.

Python

```
list1 = [1, 2, 3]
list2 = [4, 5]
list1.extend(list2)
print(list1)  # Output: [1, 2, 3, 4, 5]
```

5.3: Common List Operations (Optional for Day 3)

Lists in Python come with a variety of built-in functions that make working with them efficient. Here are some commonly used operations:

1. Finding the Length:

The `len(list)` function returns the number of elements in a list.

Python

```python
fruits = ["apple", "banana", "cherry"]
list_length = len(fruits)
print(list_length)   # Output: 3
```

2. Finding the Index:

The `list.index(element)` method returns the index of the first occurrence of a specified element in the list.

Python

```python
numbers = [10, 20, 30, 20, 50]
element_index = numbers.index(20)
print(element_index)   # Output: 1
```

3. Checking Element Existence:

The `in` operator allows you to check if an element exists in a list. It returns `True` if the element is found, and `False` otherwise.

Python

```python
colors = ["red", "green", "blue"]
is_present = "green" in colors
print(is_present)   # Output: True
```

4. Sorting:

The `list.sort()` method sorts the elements of a list in ascending order (you can optionally specify `reverse=True` for descending order). This modification happens in-place, meaning it sorts the original list.

Python

```python
numbers = [3, 1, 4, 5, 2]
numbers.sort()
print(numbers)  # Output: [1, 2, 3, 4, 5]
```

5. Reversing:

The `list.reverse()` method reverses the order of elements in a list. Similar to `sort()`, this is an in-place modification.

Python

```python
fruits = ["apple", "banana", "cherry"]
fruits.reverse()
print(fruits)   # Output: ["cherry", "banana", "apple"]
```

Remember:

`sort()` and `reverse()` modify the original list. If you want to preserve the original list, create a copy using slicing (we'll cover slicing in a later section) before sorting or reversing.

These are just a few of the many list operations available in Python. As you progress in your Python journey, you'll encounter more advanced techniques for working with lists.

5.4: Looping Through Lists

Lists and loops are a powerful combination in Python. Loops allow you to iterate through each element in a list, performing operations or calculations on them. This is essential for processing and manipulating list data.

Using for loops:

The `for` loop is the go-to choice for iterating through elements in a list. Here's the basic syntax:

```Python
for element in list_name:
    # Code to be executed for each element
```

The `for` keyword initiates the loop.

`element` is a temporary variable that takes on the value of each item in the list during each iteration.

`list_name` is the list you want to iterate through.

The indented code block represents the statements that will be executed for each element in the list.

Example:

```Python
fruits = ["apple", "banana", "cherry"]
```

```
for fruit in fruits:
  print(fruit)
```

This code iterates through the `fruits` list, assigning each fruit name to the variable `fruit` in each loop iteration. Inside the loop, we simply print the current fruit. This will output:

```
apple
banana
cherry
```

Looping with Index (Optional):

You can also use the `enumerate` function to get both the index and the element value during each iteration of the loop.

Python

```
fruits = ["apple", "banana", "cherry"]
for index, fruit in enumerate(fruits):
  print(index, fruit)
```

Here, `enumerate` returns an enumerate object, which is essentially a list of tuples where each tuple contains the index and the corresponding element from the original list. This code will output:

```
0 apple
1 banana
2 cherry
```

Common Looping Tasks:

Accessing and Processing Elements: Inside the loop, you can access the current element using the loop variable and perform operations on it.

Modifying Elements: If the list is mutable (like most lists you'll work with), you can change the elements within the loop.

Building New Lists: You can use a loop to iterate through a list and create a new list based on specific conditions or calculations.

In the next section (optional for Day 4), we'll introduce list comprehensions, a concise and powerful way to create new lists based on existing ones.

5.5: List Comprehensions (Optional for Day 4)

List comprehensions provide a concise and powerful way to create new lists based on existing lists in Python. They offer a compact alternative to traditional for loops for creating new lists.

Basic Syntax:

```Python
new_list = [expression for item in iterable if
condition]
```

new_list: This variable will store the newly created list.

expression: This is the expression that will be applied to each element in the iterable (usually the original list).

`item`: This variable represents each item during iteration through the iterable.

`iterable`: This is the list (or other iterable object) that you're iterating through.

`condition` **(optional):** This is an optional condition that can be used to filter elements from the resulting list. Only elements for which the condition evaluates to `True` will be included in the new list.

Example:

Python

```python
numbers = [1, 2, 3, 4, 5]
squares = [number * number for number in numbers]
print(squares)  # Output: [1, 4, 9, 16, 25]
```

In this example, the list comprehension creates a new list named `squares` that contains the squares of each number in the `numbers` list. The expression `number * number` squares each element, and the loop iterates through the `numbers` list. There's no condition in this case, so all elements are included in the new list.

Benefits of List Comprehensions:

Conciseness: List comprehensions often express complex list creation logic in a single line of code, making them more readable and maintainable compared to for loops in some cases.

Versatility: They can be used for various tasks like filtering, mapping (applying a function to each element), and creating new lists based on conditions.

More Examples:

Filtering elements:

Python

```python
positive_numbers = [number for number in numbers
if number > 0]
print(positive_numbers)   # Output: [1, 2, 3, 4,
5]
```

Extracting specific elements:

Python

```python
strings = ["apple", "banana", "cherry", "10"]
string_lengths = [len(s) for s in strings if
isinstance(s, str)]  # Filter non-strings
print(string_lengths)  # Output: [5, 6, 6]
```

List comprehensions become more powerful as you combine these concepts to create complex new lists with filtering and transformations.

Chapter 6

Automating Tasks with Loops and Conditionals (Day 4)

Welcome back, Python champions! In the previous chapters, you conquered variables, data types, operators, control flow with conditional statements and loops, functions, and working with lists. This chapter dives deeper into the power of loops and conditional statements, the dynamic duo of Python for automating repetitive tasks and making your programs intelligent.

6.1: Review of Loops and Conditionals

In our journey towards Python mastery, we've previously encountered two fundamental concepts: loops and conditional statements. Let's refresh our memory on these building blocks before diving into their combined power for automating tasks.

Loops:

Loops allow you to execute a block of code repeatedly until a specific condition is met. They are ideal for automating repetitive tasks and processing sequences of elements.

`for` **loops:** These loops iterate through a sequence of elements, like a list, string, or tuple. In each iteration, a loop variable takes on the value of the current element.

`while` **loops:** These loops continue executing a block of code as long as a condition is true. Once the condition becomes false, the loop terminates.

Conditional Statements:

Conditional statements control the flow of your program's execution based on certain conditions. They allow your program to make decisions and execute different code blocks depending on whether conditions are true or false.

`if` **statements:** These are the foundation of conditional statements. An `if` statement evaluates a condition, and if it's true, the code block following the `if` statement is executed.

`elif` **(else if) statements:** These are optional statements that can be chained after an `if` statement to check additional conditions if the original `if` condition was false.

`else` **statements:** The `else` statement provides an optional block of code to execute if none of the previous conditions in `if` or `elif` statements were true.

The Synergy of Loops and Conditionals:

By combining loops and conditional statements, you create powerful programs that can automate tasks, make decisions based on data, and interact with the world in an intelligent way. In the following sections, we'll delve deeper into the intricacies of `for` and `while` loops, explore nested loops, and see how to effectively combine them with conditional statements for real-world problem-solving in Python.

6.2: The for Loop in Depth

The `for` loop is a fundamental construct in Python that allows you to iterate through a sequence of elements in an automated way.

It's a versatile tool for processing elements in lists, strings, tuples, and other iterables.

Understanding the Basics:

The general syntax of a `for` loop is:

Python

```
for element in iterable:
# Code to be executed for each element
```

`for`: This keyword initiates the loop.

`element`: This variable name represents each item in the sequence during each iteration of the loop. You can choose any valid variable name here.

`iterable`: This is the sequence you want to iterate through. It can be a list, string, tuple, or any object that can be unpacked into a sequence of elements.

Indented code block: The indented block of code following the colon (`:`) represents the statements that will be executed for each element in the sequence.

Example:

Python

```
fruits = ["apple", "banana", "cherry"]
for fruit in fruits:
  print(fruit)
```

In this example, the loop iterates through the `fruits` list. In each iteration, the variable `fruit` takes on the value of the current fruit name ("apple", "banana", and then "cherry"). The indented code block simply prints the current fruit name.

Iterating Over a Range of Numbers:

The `for` loop can also be used to iterate over a sequence of numbers generated by the `range()` function. This is useful for scenarios where you want to perform a specific action a certain number of times.

Python

```python
for number in range(1, 6):    # Starts from 1
(inclusive) and excludes 6 (exclusive)
    print(number)
```

Here, the `range(1, 6)` function generates a sequence of numbers from 1 to 5 (excluding 6). The loop iterates through this sequence, assigning the current number to the variable `number` in each iteration, and then prints the number.

Using `break` **and** `continue`

`break`**:** The `break` statement allows you to prematurely exit a loop if a specific condition is met. This can be helpful for situations where you no longer need to continue iterating through the sequence.

Python

```python
for number in range(1, 11):
if number == 5:
```

```
break  # Exit the loop when number is 5
print(number)
```

In this example, the loop iterates from 1 to 10. However, if the current number is 5, the `break` statement is encountered, and the loop terminates even though there are more numbers in the range.

`continue`: The `continue` statement skips the remaining code in the current iteration of the loop and jumps to the next iteration. It's useful when you want to conditionally skip processing a particular element but still continue iterating through the entire sequence.

Python

```
for number in range(1, 11):
if number % 2 == 0:  # Skip even numbers
continue
print(number)
```

Here, the loop iterates from 1 to 10. If the current number is even, the `continue` statement is executed, skipping the `print(number)` statement for that iteration and moving on to the next odd number in the sequence.

Remember:

Indentation is crucial in Python loops. The code block to be executed for each iteration must be properly indented.

Using `break` and `continue` effectively can make your loops more efficient and avoid unnecessary iterations.

6.3: The while Loop in Depth

The `while` loop is another essential looping construct in Python. It allows you to execute a block of code repeatedly as long as a specified condition remains `True`. While `for` loops excel at iterating through a predetermined sequence, `while` loops provide more flexibility for situations where the number of iterations is unknown beforehand, or the loop needs to continue based on a dynamic condition.

Understanding the Syntax:

The general syntax of a `while` loop is:

Python

```python
while condition:
    # Code to be executed as long as the condition
    is True
```

`while`: This keyword initiates the loop.

`condition`: This is a Boolean expression that determines whether the loop continues to execute. The loop keeps iterating as long as the `condition` evaluates to `True`. Once the condition becomes `False`, the loop terminates.

Indented code block: Similar to `for` loops, the indented block of code following the colon (`:`) represents the statements that will be executed repeatedly as long as the condition is `True`.

Example:

Python

```python
guess_count = 0
guess_limit = 5
secret_number = 7

while guess_count < guess_limit:
  guess = int(input("Guess a number between 1 and
10: "))
  guess_count += 1
  if guess == secret_number:
    print("Congratulations, you guessed it!")
    break  # Exit the loop if guess is correct
  else:
    print("Try again.")

if guess_count == guess_limit:  # Optional check
after the loop terminates
    print("Sorry, you ran out of guesses. The
number was", secret_number)
```

In this example, the loop simulates a guessing game. The loop continues as long as guess_count is less than guess_limit (5). Inside the loop, the user is prompted for a guess, and the guess is compared to the secret number. If the guess is correct, the loop exits using break. An optional if statement after the loop checks if the guess limit was reached without a successful guess.

Key Points:

The `while` loop is ideal for situations where the number of iterations is not predetermined or depends on a changing condition.

It's essential to ensure that the condition within the `while` loop eventually evaluates to `False` to prevent an infinite loop. Incorporate logic within the loop to modify the condition or introduce a maximum number of iterations to avoid this.

Similar to `for` loops, indentation is crucial for defining the code block that executes within the loop.

6.4: Nested Loops

Nested loops involve placing one loop inside another loop. This creates a more intricate execution flow, allowing you to iterate through multiple sequences or perform operations multiple times for each element in an outer loop. Nested loops are particularly useful for tasks that require working with multidimensional data structures like matrices or grids.

Understanding Nested Loops:

Imagine a box of chocolates. An outer loop can iterate through each row of chocolates in the box, and an inner loop can iterate through each chocolate within that row to process them individually.

```python
Python

rows = 3  # Number of rows
columns = 4  # Number of chocolates in each row

for i in range(rows):  # Outer loop for rows
```

```python
for j in range(columns):    # Inner loop for
chocolates in each row
print(f"Row {i+1}, Chocolate {j+1}")  # Print row
and chocolate number
```

In this example, the outer loop (`for i in range(rows)`) iterates three times (once for each row). Within each iteration of the outer loop, the inner loop (`for j in range(columns)`) iterates four times (once for each chocolate in that row). The nested loops allow us to access and process each chocolate systematically.

Real-World Applications:

Nested loops have various applications in Python programming. Here are some examples:

Matrix operations: Multiplying matrices or performing other mathematical operations on multidimensional arrays often involves nested loops to iterate through each element.

2D games: Nested loops can be used to create game grids, update the positions of game elements, and handle player interactions within the game world.

Data processing: Iterating through nested structures like lists of lists or dictionaries of lists can be effectively done using nested loops.

Important Considerations:

Indentation: Nested loops rely heavily on proper indentation to define the inner and outer loop structures. Ensure proper indentation to avoid errors.

Complexity: While nested loops are powerful, they can add complexity to your code. Strive to break down complex nested logic into smaller, more manageable functions if necessary.

6.5: Looping with enumerate (Optional for Day 4)

We previously encountered the `enumerate` function in Chapter 5. It's a useful tool that can enhance your control over loops. Recall that `enumerate` takes an iterable (like a list) and returns an enumerate object, which is essentially a list of tuples. Each tuple contains an index (starting from 0) and the corresponding element from the original iterable.

Using enumerate for Index Access:

Python

```python
fruits = ["apple", "banana", "cherry"]
for index, fruit in enumerate(fruits):
 print(f"Index: {index}, Fruit: {fruit}")
```

In this example, the `enumerate` function is used within the `for` loop. Instead of just iterating through the fruit names, the loop unpacks the enumerate object, assigning the index to the variable `index` and the fruit name to `fruit` in each iteration. This provides you with both the index and the element during every loop iteration.

Benefits of enumerate:

Improved Readability: Using `enumerate` can sometimes make loop code more readable, especially when you need to process both the element and its corresponding index within the sequence.

Avoiding Counter Variables: In some cases, `enumerate` can eliminate the need for a separate counter variable within the loop, making the code more concise.

Example: Creating a List with Index Manipulation

Python

```python
numbers = [10, 20, 30, 40]
doubled_numbers = []
for i, number in enumerate(numbers):
doubled_numbers.append(number * 2)
# OR a more concise approach using enumerate
directly (assuming i starts at 0)
# doubled_numbers.append(number * 2 if i % 2 != 0
else number)  # Double only even indexed numbers

print(doubled_numbers)   # Output: [20, 20, 60,
40]
```

Here, we use `enumerate` to create a new list `doubled_numbers` that contains the original numbers doubled. The even-numbered index check in the second approach demonstrates how you can leverage the index information obtained from `enumerate` for more complex conditional operations within the loop.

Remember: enumerate is a versatile tool that can streamline your loops and enhance readability when working with sequences and their corresponding indices in Python.

6.6: Putting Loops and Conditionals Together

The true power of loops and conditional statements emerges when you combine them to make intelligent decisions within your programs. This fusion allows you to automate tasks, analyze data, and create interactive programs that respond to user input or changing conditions.

Conditional Statements Within Loops

You can effectively use conditional statements (like if, elif, and else) within loops to control which elements are processed or what actions are taken based on specific criteria.

Example: Finding Even Numbers

Python

```
numbers = [10, 4, 7, 9, 2, 8]
even_numbers = []
for number in numbers:
if number % 2 == 0:  # Check if even
even_numbers.append(number)
print(even_numbers)  # Output: [10, 4, 2, 8]
```

Here, the loop iterates through the numbers list. Inside the loop, an if statement checks if the current number is even using the modulo operator (%). If the condition is True (the number is even), the number is appended to the even_numbers list. This demonstrates how you can filter elements based on a condition within a loop.

More Complex Logic with `elif` **and** `else`

Python

```
grades = ["A", "B", "C", "D", "F"]
grade_counts = {"A": 0, "B": 0, "C": 0, "D": 0,
"F": 0}
for grade in grades:
if grade == "A":
grade_counts["A"] += 1
elif grade == "B":
grade_counts["B"] += 1
elif grade == "C":
grade_counts["C"] += 1
else:   # Handles D and F (can be further improved
for clarity)
        grade_counts[grade] += 1   # Could use a
separate elif for D

print(grade_counts)   # Output: {'A': 1, 'B': 1,
'C': 1, 'D': 1, 'F': 1} (assuming the sample
grades)
```

In this example, the loop iterates through a list of grades. We use a combination of `if`, `elif`, and `else` statements to categorize each grade into its corresponding count within the `grade_counts` dictionary. The `else` block handles grades that are not A, B, or C (which could be further improved for readability by adding a separate `elif` for "D" if desired).

Nested Loops with Conditionals

You can combine nested loops with conditional statements to create even more intricate programs. Imagine a 2D grid where you want to process elements based on certain conditions. Nested loops provide the structure for iterating through the grid, and conditionals allow you to make decisions about each element.

Real-World Applications:

Data Analysis: Iterating through data sets and applying conditions to filter or group data is a common use case for loops and conditionals.

User Input Validation: Validating user input to ensure it meets specific criteria often involves loops and conditional statements.

Game Development: The core logic of many games relies on loops and conditionals to update game states, handle player interactions, and control game mechanics.

By effectively combining loops and conditional statements, you empower your Python programs to handle complex tasks, make data-driven decisions, and interact with the world in an intelligent way. As you progress in your Python journey, you'll encounter even more creative applications of these fundamental control flow mechanisms.

Chapter 7

Introduction to User Input and Strings (Day 5) covers the fundamentals of getting user input and working with strings in Python.

7.1: User Input

In Python, the `input()` function allows your programs to interact with users and get information from them. This function pauses the program's execution and displays a message (prompt) on the screen, waiting for the user to type in some text. Once the user presses Enter, the user's input is captured as a string and returned by the `input()` function.

Here's the basic syntax:

Python

```python
user_input = input("Enter your name: ")
```

`"Enter your name: "` This is the prompt displayed to the user, instructing them on what information to provide.

`user_input` This variable stores the user's entered text as a string.

Example:

Python

```python
name = input("What is your name? ")

age = int(input("How old are you? "))   # We'll
cover type conversion in later chapters


print(f"Hello, {name}! You are {age} years old.")
```

In this example, the program prompts the user for their name and then for their age. The `input()` function captures the user's input for both questions and stores them in the variables `name` and `age` (notice we convert the age input to an integer using `int()` for further processing). An f-string is then used to greet the user by name and age.

Key Points:

The `input()` function always returns a string, even if the user enters numbers.

You can use string methods (covered later in the course) to manipulate the user input if needed (e.g., converting to uppercase or numbers).

The `input()` function is a powerful tool for creating interactive programs that respond to user input.

7.2: String Fundamentals

Strings are the fundamental building blocks for textual data in Python. They represent sequences of characters enclosed in either single quotes (') or double quotes ("). These characters can be letters, numbers, symbols, or spaces. Mastering how to work with strings is essential for various programming tasks, from user input to data manipulation and output formatting.

Creating Strings:

You can create strings by enclosing characters within single or double quotes. The choice between single or double quotes is mainly a matter of preference or readability, as long as the quotes are used consistently within the string.

Python

```
message1 = 'Hello, world!'  # Single quotes

message2 = "This is another string."  # Double quotes
```

Accessing Characters in Strings:

Strings in Python are ordered sequences, meaning characters have a specific position (index) within the string. Indexing starts from 0, so the first character is at index 0, the second character at index 1, and so on. You can access individual characters using their index within square brackets [].

Python

```
name = "Alice"

first_letter = name[0]   # A (accessing the character at index 0)

last_letter = name[-1]   # e (accessing the last character using negative indexing)
```

String Slicing:

String slicing extracts a sub-section of characters from a string. You specify the starting and ending index (separated by a colon) within square brackets. The ending index position is exclusive, meaning it's not included in the sliced string.

```python
greeting = "Hello, world!"

hello = greeting[0:5]    # Hello (extracts characters from index 0 to 4 (excluding 5))

world = greeting[7:]    # world (extracts characters from index 7 to the end)
```

String Concatenation:

The + operator is used to concatenate (join) multiple strings together. This creates a new string by combining the characters of the original strings.

```python
first_name = "Alice"

last_name = "Smith"

full_name = first_name + " " + last_name

print(full_name)  # Output: Alice Smith
```

Immutability of Strings:

An important concept to remember is that strings in Python are immutable. This signifies that once a string is created, its content cannot be modified directly. Assigning a new value to a variable containing a string creates a new string object, rather than changing the original string.

Python

```python
message = "Hello, world!"

# message[0] = 'J'  # This will cause an error!
Strings are immutable
```

In this example, attempting to modify the first character of `message` using indexing will result in an error because strings are immutable. To create a new string with the desired change, you can use string concatenation or f-strings (covered later).

String Length:

The `len()` function determines the length (number of characters) in a string.

Python

```python
name = "Bob"

name_length = len(name)

print(f"The name '{name}' has {name_length} characters.")
```

Escape Sequences:

Escape sequences are special character combinations within strings that represent non-printable characters or modify how the string is interpreted. These sequences start with a backslash () followed by a character or code to specify the desired behavior.

Here are some common escape sequences:

\n: Newline (creates a new line)

\t: Horizontal tab

\\: Backslash

': Single quote (within a single-quoted string)

": Double quote (within a double-quoted string)

```
Python

message  =   "Hello,\nworld!  This  string  has  a
newline."

print(message)
```

7.3: Accessing Characters in Strings

In Python, strings are like sequences of characters, and you can access individual characters using their index positions. This section dives deeper into how to retrieve characters from strings using indexing and negative indexing.

Indexing for Character Access:

Strings in Python are ordered sequences, meaning each character has a designated position (index) within the string.

Indexing starts from 0. The first character is at index 0, the second character at index 1, and so on.

You can access individual characters using their index within square brackets [].

Python

```
name = "Charlie"

first_letter = name[0]    # 'C' (accessing the
character at index 0)

third_letter = name[2]    # 'r' (accessing the
character at index 2)
```

Negative Indexing:

Python also supports negative indexing for strings.

Negative indices start from the end of the string at index -1 (the last character) and continue backwards.

The index -1 refers to the last character, -2 to the second-last character, and so on.

Python

```
last_letter = name[-1]  # 'e' (accessing the last
character using -1)
```

```python
second_last_letter = name[-2]    # 'l' (accessing
the second-last character using -2)
```

Slicing for Substrings:

String slicing (covered in previous sections) allows you to extract a sub-section of characters from a string.

While not directly related to accessing single characters, it's worth mentioning here as it's a common operation when working with substrings within strings.

You specify the starting and ending index (separated by a colon) within square brackets []. Remember, the ending index is exclusive (not included) in the sliced string.

Python

```python
greeting = "Hello, world!"

hello = greeting[0:5]    # "Hello" (extracts
characters from index 0 to 4 (excluding 5))
```

Example: Traversing a String

Python

```python
name = "Alice"

for i in range(len(name)):
```

```
print(f"Character at index {i}: {name[i]}")
```

This code iterates through the string `name` using a loop. It calculates the string length using `len(name)` and iterates from 0 to length-1 (to account for zero-based indexing). Inside the loop, the character at the current index `i` is accessed using `name[i]`.

Key Points:

Indexing provides a way to access specific characters within a string.

Positive indexing starts from 0, and negative indexing starts from -1 (the last character).

Remember that the ending index in slicing is exclusive.

Use caution when using negative indexes outside the valid range (less than -len(string)) as it will result in an error.

7.4: String Slicing

String slicing is a fundamental technique in Python for extracting substrings from a string. It allows you to target specific sections of characters within a string and create new strings based on your needs.

Syntax:

String slicing uses square brackets `[]` with a colon separating the starting and ending indices.

Python

```python
string = "Hello, world!"

substring = string[start:end:step]
```

`start`: This is the index of the first character to include in the substring (inclusive). If omitted, it defaults to 0 (the beginning of the string).

`end`: This is the index of the first character to exclude from the substring (exclusive). If omitted, it defaults to the entire string length.

`step` (optional): This argument specifies the step size for including characters within the slice. A step value of 1 (the default) includes every character. Values greater than 1 will include every nth character.

Extracting Substrings:

You can extract substrings by specifying the starting and ending indices within the square brackets.

Python

```python
greeting = "Hello, world!"

hello = greeting[0:5]    # "Hello" (extracts characters from index 0 to 4 (excluding 5))

world = greeting[7:]    # "world!" (extracts characters from index 7 to the end)
```

Omitting Indices:

If you omit the starting index, the slice starts from the beginning (index 0).

If you omit the ending index, the slice goes up to the end of the string.

```Python
message = "Welcome to Python!"

first_word = message[:6]   # "Welcome"

last_part = message[14:]   # "Python!"
```

Negative Indexing:

You can also use negative indices for slicing, starting from the end of the string.

-1 refers to the last character, -2 to the second-last character, and so on.

```Python
name = "Alice"

last_letter = name[-1]    # 'e' (extracting the last character using -1)

second_part = name[:-2]   # "Al" (extracting all characters except the last two)
```

Step Size in Slicing:

The `step` argument in slicing allows you to extract every nth character within the specified range.

A step value of 1 (the default) includes every character.

A step value of 2 includes every other character, and so on.

```python
Python

sentence = "Python is fun!"

every_other = sentence[::2]    # "Pto siu!" (extracts every other character)

first_three = sentence[::3]   # "Pti" (extracts every third character)
```

Key Points:

String slicing provides a versatile way to extract substrings from strings.

Remember that the ending index is exclusive in slicing.

Negative indices start from the end of the string.

The `step` argument allows you to control which characters are included in the slice based on a specified interval.

7.5: String Concatenation

String concatenation is the process of joining multiple strings together to create a new string. Python provides a straightforward method for combining strings using the + operator.

Creating a New String:

Python

```python
first_name = "Alice"

last_name = "Smith"

full_name = first_name + " " + last_name

print(full_name)  # Output: Alice Smith
```

In this example, the + operator is used to concatenate three strings: `first_name`, a space, and `last_name`. The result is a new string stored in the variable `full_name`.

Concatenating Variables and Strings:

You can concatenate strings with variables that contain strings.

Python

```python
greeting = "Hello, "

name = "Bob"

personalized_greeting = greeting + name + "!"
```

```
print(personalized_greeting)     # Output: Hello,
Bob!
```

Concatenation with Multiple Strings:

The + operator can be chained together to concatenate multiple strings.

Python

```
message = "It's " + str(3) + " o'clock!"    #
Convert the number 3 to a string using str()

print(message)  # Output: It's 3 o'clock!
```

Important Considerations:

While string concatenation is simple, it can create a large number of temporary strings if used excessively. In such cases, string formatting methods (like f-strings covered later) can be more efficient for readability and memory usage.

Concatenating strings with numbers directly will result in an error. You'll need to convert the number to a string using the `str()` function before concatenation.

7.6: Immutability of Strings

Strings in Python are considered immutable. This means that once a string is created, its content cannot be modified directly. This concept is essential to understand when working with strings in Python to avoid confusion and unexpected behavior.

Understanding Immutability:

Imagine a string as a sentence written on a piece of paper. You can't rewrite the sentence on the same paper to make changes. Instead, you would need to create a new piece of paper and write the modified sentence on it.

Similarly, in Python, when you try to modify a string, Python doesn't change the original string object. Instead, it creates a new string object with the desired changes and assigns it to a new variable or modifies the reference of an existing variable.

Example:

```python
Python

message = "Hello, world!"


# Attempting to modify a character directly

try:

message[0] = 'J'

except TypeError as e:

print("Error:", e)

print("Strings are immutable. You cannot modify characters directly.")
```

This code attempts to change the first character of `message` from 'H' to 'J' using indexing. However, this will result in a `TypeError` because strings are immutable.

Creating a New String:

To modify the content, you need to create a new string with the changes and assign it to a new variable or modify the reference of an existing variable.

Python

```python
new_message = 'J' + message[1:]

print(new_message)  # Output: Jello, world!
```

Here, we create a new string `new_message` by concatenating the letter 'J' with the sliced part of `message` from index 1 onwards (excluding the first character 'H').

Key Points:

Immutability of strings is a fundamental concept in Python.

Attempting to modify a string directly will result in an error.

To create a modified version, create a new string with the desired changes.

String methods (covered later) provide ways to manipulate strings without directly modifying the original string.

7.7: Built-in String Methods

Python offers a rich collection of built-in string methods that provide powerful ways to manipulate and work with strings. These methods operate on strings without modifying the original string (remember immutability) and return a new string object with the desired transformation.

Here are some commonly used string methods:

`upper()`: Converts the string to uppercase.

Python

```
message = "Hello, world!"

uppercase_message = message.upper()

print(uppercase_message)   # Output: HELLO, WORLD!
```

`lower()`: Converts the string to lowercase.

Python

```
name = "ALICE"

lowercase_name = name.lower()

print(lowercase_name)   # Output: alice
```

`strip()`: Removes leading and trailing whitespaces from the string.

Python

```python
greeting = "   Hello, world!    "

stripped_greeting = greeting.strip()

print(stripped_greeting)  # Output: Hello, world!
```

find(substring): Returns the index of the first occurrence of a substring within the string, or -1 if not found.

Python

```python
message = "Welcome to Python programming!"

index = message.find("Python")

print(f"The word 'Python' starts at index: {index}")  # Output: The word 'Python' starts at index: 8
```

replace(old, new): Replaces all occurrences of a substring with a new substring.

Python

```python
old_sentence = "This is a string with banana."

new_sentence = old_sentence.replace("banana", "apple")
```

```
print(new_sentence)    # Output: This is a string
with apple.
```

split(separator): Splits the string into a list based on a specified separator (delimiter). If no separator is provided, it splits by whitespace by default.

Python

```
csv_line = "name,age,city"

data_list = csv_line.split(",")

print(data_list)      # Output: ['name', 'age',
'city']
```

join(iterable): Joins the elements of an iterable (like a list) into a string using a specified separator.

Python

```
names = ["Alice", "Bob", "Charlie"]

joined_string = " & ".join(names)

print(joined_string)    # Output: Alice & Bob &
Charlie
```

isalnum(): Checks if all characters in the string are alphanumeric (letters and numbers).

Python

```python
alphanumeric_string = "Hello123"

print(alphanumeric_string.isalnum())   # Output: True
```

isalpha(): Checks if all characters in the string are alphabetic (letters).

Python

```python
alphabetic_string = "Python"

print(alphabetic_string.isalpha())   # Output: True
```

isdigit(): Checks if all characters in the string are digits (numbers).

Python

```python
digit_string = "12345"

print(digit_string.isdigit())  # Output: True
```

`isspace()`: Checks if all characters in the string are whitespaces.

Python

```
whitespace_string = "    "

print(whitespace_string.isspace())    # Output: True
```

These are just a few examples, and there are many more string methods available in Python's library. As you progress in your Python journey, you'll encounter more methods that cater to specific string manipulation tasks.

Chapter 8

Taking Control of Your Code Flow (Day 5 & 6)

This chapter likely delves deeper into using loops and conditionals to achieve more complex program behavior. Here are some potential areas of focus:

Nested Loops: Nested loops involve using loops within other loops. This allows you to iterate through multi-dimensional data structures (like grids or matrices) or perform operations on elements within sequences based on additional criteria.

Loop Control Statements: You might explore statements like `break` and `continue` that can be used to modify the flow of loops. `break` exits the loop prematurely, while `continue` skips the current iteration and moves to the next.

Advanced Conditional Logic: The chapter might introduce concepts like using logical operators (`and`, `or`, `not`) to combine conditions within `if` statements for more intricate decision-making.

Real-world Applications: Examples might showcase how loops and conditionals are used in practical scenarios, such as data analysis (iterating through data sets and applying conditions), user input validation (ensuring user input meets specific criteria), and game development (controlling game mechanics and state changes).

Learning by Doing:

The best way to solidify your understanding of loops and conditionals is through practice. Here are some tips:

Review Code Examples: The chapter likely provides code examples demonstrating loop and conditional usage. Work through these examples, understand the logic, and try modifying them to explore different scenarios.

Write Your Own Practice Programs: Challenge yourself by creating mini-programs that utilize loops and conditionals. Start with simple tasks like finding even numbers in a list or guessing a random number within a range. Gradually increase the complexity as you gain confidence.

Explore Online Coding Platforms: Many online platforms offer interactive coding environments where you can experiment with Python code and receive instant feedback. This can be a valuable tool for practicing loops and conditionals in a safe and engaging way.

By effectively combining loops and conditional statements, you empower your Python programs to automate tasks, make data-driven decisions, and interact with the world in an intelligent manner. As you progress through your Python journey, these fundamental control flow mechanisms will become the building blocks for creating more complex and versatile programs.

8.1 Breaks and Continues: Controlling Loop Execution

In Python loops (`for` and `while`), you may sometimes need to alter the default execution flow. The `break` and `continue` statements provide mechanisms to control how loops iterate and when they terminate.

The `break` Statement:

The `break` statement prematurely exits the loop, regardless of whether the loop condition is still `True`.

Once `break` is executed, control jumps out of the loop, and the program proceeds to the code following the loop.

Python

```python
numbers = [10, 20, 30, 40, 5, 6]

for number in numbers:

 if number == 20:

 print(f"Found {number}! Breaking the loop.")

 break

 print(f"Checking: {number}")
```

In this example, the loop iterates through the `numbers` list. The `if` condition checks for the number 20. If found, the `break` statement is executed, terminating the loop even though there are remaining elements in the list. The program then continues with the code after the loop.

The `continue` Statement:

The `continue` statement skips the current iteration of the loop and jumps to the next iteration.

The remaining code within the current iteration is not executed after `continue`.

Python

```python
fruits = ["apple", "banana", "cherry", "orange", "kiwi"]
```

```python
for fruit in fruits:

if fruit == "banana":

print(f"Skipping {fruit}")

continue

print(f"Processing: {fruit}")
```

Here, the loop iterates through the `fruits` list. When it encounters "banana", the `continue` statement skips processing it and moves on to the next iteration ("cherry"). This demonstrates how `continue` can be used to selectively process elements within a loop.

Key Points:

`break` exits the loop entirely.

`continue` skips the current iteration and moves to the next.

Use these statements strategically to control loop execution based on your program's logic.

8.2 Functions with Return Values: Sending Data Back from Functions

In previous chapters, you explored how to define and use functions in Python. Functions are reusable blocks of code that perform specific tasks. We saw that functions can take arguments (inputs) but didn't explicitly return any data (output) from the function itself.

Introducing Return Values:

Functions can optionally return a value using the `return` statement. This value becomes the output of the function call and can be assigned to a variable or used in expressions.

The `return` statement can be used anywhere within the function's body. Once a `return` statement is executed, the function immediately terminates, and control returns to the caller.

Python

```python
def calculate_area(length, width):

    area = length * width

    return area  # Returning the calculated area



rectangle_length = 5

rectangle_width = 3

total_area    =    calculate_area(rectangle_length, rectangle_width)

print(f"The    area    of    the    rectangle    is: {total_area}")
```

In this example, the `calculate_area` function takes two arguments (length and width) and calculates the area. The `return area` statement sends the calculated area back to the caller, where it's stored in the variable `total_area`.

Using Return Values:

Returned values from functions can be used in various ways:

Assigned to variables for further processing.

Used directly in expressions.

Passed as arguments to other functions.

Python

```python
def is_even(number):

  if number % 2 == 0:

return True

else:

return False  # Returning a boolean value


user_number = int(input("Enter a number: "))

if is_even(user_number):

  print(f"{user_number} is an even number.")
```

```
else:

    print(f"{user_number} is an odd number.")
```

Here, the `is_even` function returns a boolean value (`True` or `False`) indicating whether the number is even. The caller (the `if` statement) uses the returned value to determine which code block to execute.

Key Points:

The `return` statement allows functions to send data back to the caller.

Returned values can be of any data type (numbers, strings, lists, etc.).

Functions can optionally return no value using just `return` (without an expression). In this case, the function effectively returns `None`.

By effectively using return values, you can create well-structured and modular functions that produce meaningful outputs for your Python programs.

8.3 Building Modular Applications: Organizing Your Code into Reusable Components

As your Python programs grow in complexity, it becomes increasingly important to structure your code effectively. Modular programming is a fundamental concept that involves breaking down your code into smaller, reusable components called functions.

Benefits of Modular Programming:

Improved Readability: Well-defined functions with clear purposes make code easier to understand for both yourself and others.

Maintainability: When changes are needed, you can modify specific functions without affecting unrelated parts of your code, making maintenance more manageable.

Reusability: Functions can be reused in different parts of your program or even in other programs, reducing code duplication and promoting efficiency.

Functions as Building Blocks:

Imagine your Python program as a large building. Modular programming is like using well-defined bricks (functions) to construct this building. Each brick serves a specific purpose, and by combining them strategically, you create the desired functionality.

Example: Calculator Program

Let's consider a simple calculator program:

Python

```python
def add(x, y):

    """Adds two numbers and returns the sum."""

    return x + y
```

```python
def subtract(x, y):

    """Subtracts two numbers and returns the
difference."""

    return x - y


def multiply(x, y):

    """Multiplies two numbers and returns the
product."""

    return x * y


def divide(x, y):

    """Divides two numbers and returns the quotient
(if y != 0)."""

    if y == 0:

        return "Error: Cannot divide by zero."

    else:

        return x / y


# Get user input
```

```python
num1 = float(input("Enter the first number: "))

num2 = float(input("Enter the second number: "))


# Select operation based on user choice

operation = input("Choose an operation (+, -, *,
/): ")


# Use appropriate function based on user input

if operation == "+":

result = add(num1, num2)

elif operation == "-":

result = subtract(num1, num2)

elif operation == "*":

result = multiply(num1, num2)

elif operation == "/":

result = divide(num1, num2)

else:

result = "Invalid operation."
```

```
# Print the result

print(f"The result is: {result}")
```

In this example, the calculator functionality is divided into separate functions (`add`, `subtract`, `multiply`, and `divide`), each handling a specific mathematical operation. This makes the code more organized, readable, and easier to maintain. New operations can be added by creating new functions without modifying the existing logic.

Key Points:

Modular programming promotes code reusability and maintainability.

Functions act as building blocks for constructing complex programs.

Decomposing your program into well-defined functions improves readability and promotes better code organization.

Chapter 9

Storing Data with Lists and Tuples (Day 6 & 7) aligns with what you'd expect to find in a Python course at this stage.

Here's a summary of the key concepts:

Data Structures:

Python offers various data structures to organize and manage collections of data effectively.

This chapter focuses on lists and tuples, which are used to store ordered sequences of items.

Lists:

Lists are mutable, meaning their contents can be changed after creation.

They are created using square brackets [ ] and store items of any data type separated by commas.

Elements are accessed using zero-based indexing, allowing you to retrieve specific items by their position.

Lists provide various built-in methods for adding, removing, modifying, and iterating over elements.

Tuples:

Tuples are similar to lists but are immutable, meaning their contents cannot be modified after creation.

They are created using parentheses ().

Tuples are well-suited for data that shouldn't be changed, like coordinates or configurations.

Element access in tuples is similar to lists using index positions.

Choosing Between Lists and Tuples:

Use lists when you need to modify the data within the collection.

Use tuples when data integrity and immutability are important to prevent accidental changes.

Additional Considerations:

The chapter likely explores advanced list and tuple operations beyond basic creation and access.

It might introduce concepts like nested lists and tuple unpacking for working with multi-dimensional data structures.

Understanding these data structures is crucial for various Python programming tasks, including data analysis, working with files, and creating complex data models.

By effectively using lists and tuples, you can organize your data efficiently and manipulate it programmatically in your Python programs.

If you have any specific questions about lists, tuples, or other data structures you encounter in your Python course, feel free to ask!

9.1 Lists vs. Tuples: Understanding Mutable and Immutable Data Structures

Absolutely! Lists and tuples are both fundamental data structures in Python used for storing collections of items, but they differ in their mutability. Here's a breakdown of their key characteristics:

Lists

Mutable: Elements in a list can be changed after creation. This allows you to add, remove, or modify items within the list.

Creation: Lists are created using square brackets `[]`. Items within the brackets are separated by commas.

Example: `fruits = ["apple", "banana", "cherry"]`

Tuples

Immutable: Elements in a tuple cannot be changed after creation. Once a tuple is created, its contents are fixed.

Creation: Tuples are created using parentheses `()`. You can optionally include commas to separate items, but for single-item tuples, parentheses are mandatory to distinguish them from numeric expressions.

Example: `coordinates = (3, 5)`, `single_item_tuple = (1,)` (note the comma after the 1)

Understanding Immutability:

Think of lists like a grocery shopping list that you can update as you shop. You can add forgotten items, remove items you don't need, or change quantities.

Tuples are like a historical record, such as a list of presidents. The order and data shouldn't be modified after the record is created.

Choosing Between Lists and Tuples:

Use lists when you need to store and modify a collection of items dynamically.

Use tuples when you need to store data that shouldn't be changed and its immutability ensures data integrity. Tuples are also useful for data exchange between functions as their immutability guarantees the data remains unchanged.

Example Usage:

```python
Python

# List (mutable) - shopping list that can be
modified

shopping_list = ["bread", "milk", "eggs"]

shopping_list.append("cheese")   # Add "cheese" to
the list



# Tuple (immutable) - coordinates that shouldn't
be changed
```

```
point1 = (3, 5)  # You cannot modify point1[0] to
change the x-coordinate


# Tuple unpacking (useful for multi-valued
tuples)

colors = ("red", "green", "blue")

red, green, blue = colors  # Unpack elements into
variables
```

Key Points:

Mutability is a critical distinction between lists and tuples.

Choose the appropriate data structure based on whether you need to modify the data or not.

Tuples offer benefits in terms of data integrity and can be used effectively for data exchange between functions.

9.2 Advanced List Techniques: Slicing, Sorting, and Searching

Chapter 9 likely delves deeper into working with lists in Python, introducing techniques that go beyond basic creation and access. These techniques empower you to manipulate, transform, and analyze list data effectively.

1. Slicing:

Slicing extracts a portion of a list and creates a new list. It uses square brackets [] with a colon : to specify the starting and ending indices of the desired sublist.

Basic Slicing:

Python

```
fruits = ["apple", "banana", "cherry", "orange", "mango"]

first_two = fruits[0:2]  # Extracts elements from index 0 (inclusive) to 2 (exclusive) - ["apple", "banana"]

last_three = fruits[-3:]  # Extracts from the third element from the end (index -3) to the end - ["cherry", "orange", "mango"]
```

Advanced Slicing:

You can omit the starting or ending index to include the beginning or end of the list by default.

Slicing steps allow you to extract every nth element.

Python

```
all_but_first = fruits[1:]  # From index 1 to the end - ["banana", "cherry", "orange", "mango"]
```

```
every_other = fruits[::2]  # Extracts every other
element (starting from index 0) . - ["apple",
"cherry", "mango"]
```

2. Sorting:

The `sort()` method arranges elements in a list according to a specific order.

By default, `sort()` sorts in ascending order (smallest to largest for numbers, A-Z for strings).

You can optionally provide a `key` argument to define a custom sorting logic (e.g., sorting by length of strings).

The `sorted()` function creates a new sorted list, leaving the original list unmodified.

```
Python

numbers = [6, 2, 8, 1, 4]

numbers.sort()    # Modifies the original list
numbers: [1, 2, 4, 6, 8]

sorted_fruits = sorted(fruits, reverse=True)    #
Sorts fruits in descending order (new list)
```

3. Searching:

The `in` operator checks if a specific item exists within a list.

The `index()` method returns the index of the first occurrence of an item in the list. If the item isn't found, it raises a `ValueError`.

Python

```python
if "apple" in fruits:

print("Apple is present in the list.")

position = fruits.index("cherry")    # position
will be 2
```

Key Points:

Slicing provides a powerful way to extract and manipulate sublists.

Sorting allows you to organize list elements in a specific order.

Searching techniques help you locate items within a list.

By mastering these advanced list techniques, you can effectively process and analyze list data in your Python programs.

9.3 Building Powerful Applications: Working with Organized Data Collections

Chapter 9 likely expands on your understanding of data structures in Python, particularly focusing on how to leverage them to design effective solutions for real-world problems. This section might delve into concepts like:

Data Analysis with Lists and Tuples:

Lists and tuples can store and organize various data sets, such as sensor readings, customer information, or financial records.

You can use list operations and techniques covered earlier (slicing, sorting, searching) to analyze and extract insights from this data.

For instance, you could calculate average sensor readings, find the highest or lowest values, or search for specific customer details.

Algorithms and Data Structures:

The chapter might introduce you to fundamental algorithms, which are step-by-step problem-solving procedures. These algorithms often rely on data structures like lists and tuples to efficiently process and manipulate data.

Sorting algorithms (e.g., bubble sort, insertion sort) and searching algorithms (e.g., linear search, binary search) are classic examples. Understanding these algorithms will equip you to solve computational problems effectively.

Case Studies and Applications:

Real-world examples or case studies can solidify your grasp of how data structures are used in practice. These might involve scenarios like:

Analyzing website traffic data stored in lists to understand user behavior.

Simulating game mechanics using lists to track player inventory or game state.

Working with financial data in tuples to calculate investment returns.

Here are some additional points to consider:

Choosing the Right Data Structure: The choice of data structure (lists, tuples, dictionaries, sets) depends on the specific needs of your application. Lists and tuples excel at storing ordered sequences, while dictionaries and sets are better suited for unordered collections with unique elements or key-value pairs.

Efficiency and Scalability: As your data sets grow larger, understanding the efficiency of different operations on various data structures becomes crucial. For instance, searching a sorted list using binary search is much faster than a linear search on an unsorted list.

Data Abstraction: The chapter might introduce the concept of data abstraction, which focuses on the functionality provided by a data structure rather than its internal implementation details. This allows you to work with data structures using methods and operations without worrying about the underlying mechanics.

By effectively using lists, tuples, and other data structures along with algorithms, you can build robust and efficient Python applications that can handle and analyze various data-driven tasks.

Chapter 10

Putting It All Together: Your First Python Project (Day 7)

Congratulations! Chapter 10 likely marks a significant milestone in your Python learning journey. This chapter is probably dedicated to guiding you through the creation of your first Python project, putting all the concepts you've learned so far into practice.

Building Your First Project:

The specifics of the project will vary depending on the course you're following, but here's a general outline of what you might encounter:

1 Project Idea and Planning:

The chapter might guide you through brainstorming and selecting a project idea that aligns with your interests and leverages the skills you've acquired.

It's important to choose a project that's challenging enough to be engaging but not so complex that it becomes overwhelming.

Planning your project involves breaking it down into smaller, achievable tasks. This will make the development process more manageable.

2 Coding the Project:

You'll likely use the knowledge gained from previous chapters to write Python code for your project. This could involve:

Defining functions to encapsulate specific functionalities.

Using loops and conditional statements to control the program flow.

Working with data structures like lists, tuples, or even dictionaries (if introduced earlier) to store and manipulate data.

Taking user input (if applicable) to allow the program to interact with the user.

3 Testing and Debugging:

Testing your project involves running it with various inputs and verifying that it produces the expected outputs. This helps identify and fix any errors or bugs in your code.

Debugging is the process of locating and resolving these errors. The chapter might introduce debugging techniques like using a print statement to inspect variable values or using a debugger tool to step through your code line by line.

4 Documenting Your Project:

Well-written comments within your code improve readability and maintainability. You might be encouraged to add comments to explain your code's logic and functionality.

Some courses might suggest creating additional documentation, such as a README file, to explain the purpose of your project, how to run it, and any dependencies it might have.

Benefits of Building Your First Project:

Solidifying Your Learning: Putting your theoretical knowledge into practice through a project is a powerful way to solidify your understanding of Python concepts.

Developing Problem-Solving Skills: The process of designing, coding, testing, and debugging your project helps you develop essential problem-solving skills applicable to various coding challenges.

Building a Portfolio: Your completed project serves as a portfolio piece showcasing your Python abilities to potential employers or collaborators.

Boosting Confidence and Motivation: Successfully completing your first project can be a rewarding experience, boosting your confidence and motivation to continue learning and creating more complex Python programs.

Tips for Success:

Don't Be Afraid to Experiment: Embrace the opportunity to experiment and try different approaches while coding your project. This will enhance your learning and problem-solving skills.

Seek Help When Needed: If you encounter challenges, don't hesitate to consult your course materials, online resources, or seek help from instructors or communities.

Most Importantly, Have Fun! Learning Python should be an enjoyable experience. Approach your project with a positive attitude and focus on the satisfaction of creating something functional and engaging.

Chapter 10 marks a significant step towards becoming a proficient Python programmer. By following the guidance provided, actively participating in the project creation process, and embracing the challenges, you'll be well on your way to building more complex and impressive Python applications in the future!

10.1 Choosing a Project Idea: Applying Your Skills to a Real-World Scenario

Chapter 10 is all about putting your Python skills into action by building your first project! This section likely focuses on helping you brainstorm and choose a project idea that's both engaging and allows you to apply the concepts you've learned throughout your Python course.

Here are some key aspects to consider when selecting your project idea:

Interest and Motivation: Choose a project that excites you! If you're passionate about a particular topic, you'll be more motivated to learn and overcome challenges during the development process.

Skill Level: It's important to find a project that aligns with your current skillset. While you want to be challenged, avoid getting discouraged by something too complex.

Applying Learned Concepts: Look for a project that allows you to utilize the Python concepts you've covered in your course. This could involve working with functions, loops, conditionals, data structures (lists, tuples), and potentially user input or basic file operations (if introduced earlier).

Project Ideas to Spark Inspiration:

Simple Games: Tic-tac-toe, guessing games (number guessing, word guessing), simple text-based adventure games. These can be built using functions for game logic, loops for user interaction, and conditional statements for determining win/lose scenarios.

Data Analysis and Visualization: If your course covered working with data in lists or tuples, consider a project that analyzes a small dataset (e.g., movie ratings, weather data). You could calculate averages, find minimum/maximum values, or create basic data visualizations using libraries like `matplotlib` (external library installation might be required).

Text Manipulation Tools: Build a program that performs simple text manipulations, like counting word frequencies in a piece of text, converting text to uppercase/lowercase, or removing punctuation. This can involve using loops to iterate through characters or words in a string, and conditional statements for specific manipulations.

Number Guessing with Statistics: Expand the guessing game concept to track guesses and display statistics like the number of attempts taken and average number of guesses across multiple rounds. This involves using lists to store guesses and calculations using loops and conditional statements.

Additional Tips:

Start Small, Expand Later: It's better to begin with a smaller, well-defined project and gradually add complexity as you gain confidence.

Look for Inspiration Online: Numerous online resources showcase beginner-friendly Python project ideas. Search for tutorials or code examples that pique your interest.

Consider Coursework: Review past assignments or exercises from your course. These can be a good foundation for a project idea, allowing you to build upon the concepts you've already practiced.

Remember, the most important factor is to choose a project that excites you and allows you to showcase your Python skills. Don't be afraid to get creative and personalize your project to reflect your interests!

I hope this helps! Feel free to ask if you'd like to brainstorm specific project ideas based on your areas of interest or the concepts you've covered in your Python course.

10.2 Planning and Designing Your Project: Breaking Down the Problem into Steps

Chapter 10 continues guiding you through the exciting process of building your first Python project. This section likely emphasizes the importance of planning and designing your project before diving into the actual coding. Here's a breakdown of what you might encounter:

Why Planning is Important:

Effective planning lays the groundwork for a successful project.

By taking the time to plan and design your project upfront, you'll be able to:

Identify and Define Requirements: Clearly outline the functionalities your project should deliver. This helps ensure you're building something that meets your goals and user needs (if applicable).

Break Down the Project: Divide the overall project into smaller, more manageable tasks. This makes the development process less overwhelming and allows you to focus on specific functionalities one at a time.

Structure Your Code: Planning helps you visualize how different parts of your code will interact and how functions will be organized to achieve the desired outcome.

Steps for Project Planning and Design:

1 Refine Your Project Idea: Solidify your project idea by clearly defining its purpose and functionalities. Consider creating a user story or a brief description of what your project will do and how users will interact with it (if applicable).

2 Identify Key Features: List the main features your project will offer. Break down each feature Into smaller, more specific functionalities.

3 Outline the Program Flow: Plan the sequence of steps your program will take to achieve its goals. This might involve creating a flowchart or a simple textual description of the program's logic.

4 Identify Functions: Consider which functionalities can be encapsulated within separate functions. This promotes code reusability and modularity.

5 Design the User Interface (if applicable): If your project involves user interaction, plan how users will provide input and how the program will display output. This could involve a simple text-based interface or a more graphical interface (depending on the complexity of your project).

Additional Tips:

Use diagrams or flowcharts to visualize your project's design.

Write down pseudocode (informal code-like instructions) to represent the logic of your program.

Don't be afraid to revise your plan as you progress. Your initial plan might evolve as you delve deeper into the development process.

By following a structured planning and design approach, you'll set yourself up for success in building your first Python project. The more you plan and break down the problem into smaller steps, the smoother and more efficient the coding process will be!

If you have any specific questions about planning your project or translating your ideas into actionable steps, feel free to ask!

10.3 Implementing Your Project: Applying Your New Python Knowledge and Debugging Techniques

Chapter 10 guides you through the heart of building your first Python project! This section likely focuses on the exciting part - translating your plans and ideas into actual Python code. Here's a breakdown of what you'll probably encounter:

Putting Your Skills into Action:

This is where you'll leverage the Python concepts you've learned throughout your course to write code for your project.

Break down your project into smaller tasks and focus on implementing one functionality at a time. Refer to your project plan and design to ensure you're on the right track.

Key Concepts You Might Use:

Functions: Define functions to modularize your code and encapsulate specific functionalities. This promotes code reusability and improves readability.

Loops and Conditionals: Use loops (like `for` or `while`) to iterate through data or repeat actions based on conditions. Conditional statements (like `if`, `elif`, and `else`) allow your program to make decisions based on user input or calculations.

Data Structures: Utilize lists, tuples, or even dictionaries (if introduced earlier) to store and organize data within your program. Choose the appropriate data structure based on your project's needs.

User Input (if applicable): If your project involves interaction, use the `input()` function to get user input and incorporate it into your program logic.

Basic File I/O (if covered): If your course introduced file handling, you might explore reading data from or writing data to text files.

Debugging Your Code:

Errors and bugs are inevitable during the development process. The important aspect is identifying and resolving them effectively.

Here are some common debugging techniques:

Print Statements: Strategically placing `print` statements throughout your code allows you to inspect the values of variables at different points in your program. This can help identify where errors or unexpected behavior might be occurring.

Debuggers: Many Python IDEs (Integrated Development Environments) have built-in debuggers that enable you to step through your code line by line, examining variable values and the program's state at each step.

Error Messages: Pay close attention to error messages displayed by the Python interpreter. These messages often provide valuable clues about the location and nature of the error in your code.

Tips for Effective Coding:

Write Clean and Readable Code: Use proper indentation, meaningful variable names, and comments to explain your code's logic. This will make your code easier to understand for yourself and others.

Test Frequently: As you develop your project, write small test cases to verify that individual parts of your code are working as expected. This helps identify and fix issues early on before they snowball into larger problems.

Don't Get Discouraged: Encountering errors and bugs is a normal part of the learning process. Approach them as opportunities to improve your problem-solving skills and understanding of Python.

Remember, the key to successful implementation is to take it one step at a time, test thoroughly, and leverage debugging techniques to overcome challenges. If you get stuck, don't hesitate to consult your course materials, online resources, or seek help from instructors or communities.

I'd be happy to help with specific coding questions or debugging challenges you might encounter as you work on your project. Feel free to provide details about your project idea or the specific part of the code you're working on!

www.ingramcontent.com/pod-product-compliance
Lightning Source LLC
LaVergne TN
LVHW051737050326
832903LV00023B/972